INTERVIEWING DOESN'T HAVE TO SUCK

How To Eliminate Stress and Be Successful in Your Next Job Interview

GREG GILBERT

career compass

TABLE OF CONTENTS

WHY I WROTE THIS BOOK

Research shows that changing jobs ranks in the top ten most stressful life events. It requires us to spend time doing things that we don't usually do, and there's quite a bit of confusion about the process and the outcomes.

There are a lot of interviewing books out there. *A lot.* Some give you answers to the top 50 interview questions. Others offer a guarantee that if you follow their program, you will land your dream job. Still others treat the interview as a high-pressure sales tactic where you have to convince them that they can't live without you. Some advice works; some is just plain nonsense.

This book was written to clear up some of the confusion and misguided advice surrounding the whole process of interviewing for a job. Within is an uncomplicated approach where the goal is for you to be able to have a meaningful conversation with another person with minimal stress. Whatever the outcome of that conversation, you can maintain your integrity and your sanity!

This book will also clarify what to expect, how to prepare, how to conduct yourself, and how to follow up. This does not *guarantee* you'll get a job. If you follow the advice and do your best, it will *greatly improve your chances.* Rather than giving you a "right answer" to every question, you will learn a process for answering questions - you don't have to try to memorize 100 stock answers to interview questions that might come up. Besides, those kinds of stock answers won't work, as you'll discover in reading this book. You're not trying to "trick" people into hiring you. Being pushy doesn't work. I don't want you to do anything to compromise your integrity.

Similarly, there are some who give advice who haven't even had an interview in 20 years and are out of touch with what works in today's world. As of the writing of this book, I've interviewed as recently as 3 years ago, and have conducted interviews with others even more recently. I've been where many of you are.

Everything presented in this book is something I've learned to do for myself when interviewing for a job. Having also been a recruiter myself and having taught managers for years how to interview, the insights I'll share from the other side of the table should give you a solid understanding of what an interviewer is looking for. It is my hope that what I offer here will give you the tools you need to be confident and successful in your next job interview.

DISCLAIMERS

The stories throughout this book are true, but the names of the people and organizations have been omitted out of respect to them.

This book contains information and recommendations about job interviewing. The content of this book is for informational purposes only and is not intended as legal or counseling advice. You should contact an attorney or career counselor for advice on specific problems.

SPECIAL THANKS

No work, no matter how great or small, is done in a vacuum. I owe a tremendous debt of gratitude to several people in my life, starting with my son, Matt. Much of what you'll be reading was co-written by Matt, who helped me gather my scattered notes and use them to craft the completed text. He also designed the cover art and helped me investigate how to publish this book. Working on this together has been a labor of love. At the times that I wanted to give up, which were many, he pushed me to keep going. It's because of his creativity and tenacity that this book even exists.

I also want to thank my beautiful wife, Linda, who stuck with me through two major careers and a variety of jobs with all their ups and downs. She was the initial inspiration for this book, and the others that I hope will follow. She also served as an editor on this book. She is a true visionary and doesn't mind telling me to "put the banjo down and start writing."

Many other people have encouraged, coached, and mentored me along my career path. I can't name them all here, but I wouldn't be where I am today without so many wonderful people. I want to give a special shout out to Barb Minnis, Career Coach, who helped me find the career that I fell in love with and still love to this day. Also, special thanks to Susan Norton, Lisa Brommer, Bob Loudermilk, Gary Kral, Jan Mead, Jill Pletcher, Tim Link, and Chris Wallace for helping me along my career journey.

Greg Gilbert

CHAPTER 1.
INTERVIEWING DOESN'T HAVE TO SUCK

It was a cold Wednesday afternoon in late October, several years ago. The corporation I was working for had been searching for a new employee for a professional-level position for quite a while. Once again, I sat down to participate in a team interview session, as I had with several candidates we'd interviewed over the last three weeks. This candidate was highly qualified - he had multiple years of experience in the field, an advanced degree, and he dressed quite professionally. We were excited that we found him, and he seemed like a stand-out candidate for the position. The interview began very well as he started by sharing about his recent work experience and what he was doing now. Then we got into the heart of the interview - our specific questions for him.

"Tell us about a time when you faced a problem at work."

"That happens all the time. You know, big and small problems. You just have to deal with them as they come and find creative solutions," he responded.

We were a little perplexed by the answer. "Can you give us a specific example?"

"Like I said, I deal with them all the time, especially with our clients. I just try to find out what needs to be done and create a path going forward," he replied.

We tried asking a different question. "Why are you interested in this position with our organization?"

"Where I work is very seniority based. People around me have been there 20+ years, and I've been there 4 years. I can see what's coming. My boss isn't open to new ideas. She's a bit old fashioned, if you know what I mean. Don't get me wrong, I respect her, but she's just not keeping up with the technology changes. I was laid off a few years ago, and..."

We had to cut him off. "Yes, but *what* about *this* position interests you?"

He answered, "I want to be creative and join a team that embraces technology."

As he gave us these answers, our perception of the candidate unraveled quickly. This was just a small sampling of how the interview unfolded. Ultimately, the position went to someone else who was comparatively less qualified than him.

What happened here? Were these adequate responses? Did he really answer the questions that were asked? On the surface they might seem like they are adequate, but let me assure you, they most definitely are *not*. In fact, they are deal breakers.

Why? Well, because we didn't learn anything. He gave only vague, generalized, "textbook" answers. We learned *nothing* about *him* and *his ability* to do the job. You see, he made several assumptions. When he said problems "happen all the time," he assumed that we'd simply believe that general statement. Even if we did, he didn't really listen to the question, which was asking about a *time when he faced a problem*. He assumed that we would be satisfied with a sort of truism as a response. What we were looking for was not generalizations but rather examples from his own experience, and he couldn't name one time, even with multiple opportunities to do so. In the interviewing world, if you can't give one example, your credibility goes to zero.

Job interviews can suck. They can be stressful, confusing, even overwhelming. For most people, in fact, interviewing is a difficult, nerve-racking experience that they *dread*. Yes, even seasoned professionals, like the man in the story I just described, can have just as much trouble in an interview as someone fresh out of school. It's very common, actually.

To many, job interviews go hand in hand with anxiety. This anxiety comes from trying to figure out how to communicate what you have done or what you are capable of doing to people you don't know. Unprepared, many people try to do it on the spot and "wing it," which falls apart quickly.

It doesn't have to be this way! Most are simply unaware of how to respond in an interview, how to conduct themselves, or how to even prepare for one - not to mention that there is a lot of questionable advice floating around that isn't helping. I'm here to set the record straight. With a better understanding of the interview process and some preparation techniques, anyone can learn to do their best and set themselves up for success in a job interview.

I started out my career as an x-ray technician, working my way up several levels of management from Front-Line Supervisor to Director. For 16 years, I invested into that career, but increasingly, as I moved up, I realized that I was on the wrong path. So, with the help of a professional career counselor, I made a conscious decision to change careers. I switched to corporate training and development, which I found was a better fit with my natural talents and strengths.

I've now been working in that field for over 20 years. I've worked in community colleges, universities, aircraft manufacturing, and large corporations. I've had the opportunity to be a Human Resources Recruiter and Hiring Manager and I've conducted many interviews, just like the ones in this book. I've helped hundreds of people with their career paths, from ages 16 to 74, through classes and workshops, public presentations, group sessions, and individual career counseling. I also started several long-running Career Connections support groups and facilitated job clubs in my local Wichita, KS area, and have been a featured speaker at numerous Career Expos.

I've been on *both sides* of the interview table for many, many years. I've made plenty of mistakes along the way, and I've learned a lot. The techniques I'm now sharing in this book have helped many of the people I've worked with, from college students to blue collar workers to executive-level professionals. Based on their results and feedback, as well as my own results, these methods truly work! Now, I'm excited to share the best of what I know with you so you, too, can see that interviewing doesn't have to suck!

CHAPTER 2. JUST WHAT IS THE PURPOSE OF INTERVIEWING?

"You've got to be very careful if you don't know where you are going, because you might not get there." - Yogi Berra

So you've been looking to get a new job. Maybe you've navigated your way through the maelstrom of college and want to get started in your chosen profession. Maybe you've decided it's time to change careers and start something brand new. Maybe you've been a professional for years and you just aren't confident in your interviewing skills. No matter what your education or background may be, the process and advice I will give remains the same.

There are no shortcuts to getting a job. True, there are many ways to get to an interview. Whether you've developed your résumé and applied for a job listing, or you've reached out through networking. Résumés, portfolios, demo reels, LinkedIn profiles, and networking can get you to an interview, but only an interview can get you the job. It is the gateway to employment. But why is this interview process so crucial? While this may seem obvious to some, it's important to understand why interviewing is set up the way it is, and how it ultimately plays its part in the hiring process, in order to really get the most out of the experience.

Interviewing serves a two-fold purpose: It's a way to determine if someone is a close fit for a job, and it's a way to see if that person is a good fit with the existing team. Essentially, the employer has a problem and wants to know if you can solve it. It also serves the same purposes for you, the candidate. Both the potential employer and the candidate will be evaluating each other to see if the pairing would be a good fit or not. Each party may very well end up making an investment of time, energy, and/or money in each other, and so both want the best.

So it's all about having the right qualifications, then? Not quite. True, your qualifications likely got you the interview, but that isn't all there is to it. You see, there is a fundamental truth about hiring - *people hire people they like*. Oftentimes, people think they are the best qualified; therefore they will get the job. But, ultimately, the employer has to like you because they could be spending a lot of hours a week with you. You are presenting *yourself* just as much as your skills and experience. Consider the earlier story of the man who didn't get the job. He had all the right qualifications, but how he presented himself worked against him, and the job went to someone else.

That's not to say that you're on trial, though! Think of an interview more like a test-run. When you're looking for a new car, some of the most important things you look for are: "How well is this car going to perform? Can I afford it? Is it what I'm looking for?" These are exactly the same thoughts a potential employer is thinking about when interviewing a candidate - "How well is this person going to perform? Can I afford them? How well will they fit in?" Likewise, you'll be using this opportunity to gauge if you think this employer is even a right fit for you. "Can I do the job? Is this a place where I want to invest my time and energy? Will I be valued and appreciated for doing good work?"

By this point, you've already done all the hard work of building a résumé and filling out job applications, and now you've finally gotten a call for an interview. Let's work together to make that interview a positive experience for you!

CHAPTER 3. WHAT CAN I EXPECT IN AN INTERVIEW?

Whether you are interviewing for an entry-level job or a professional career position, much of the process remains the same. Let's start by looking at an overview of the typical interview process, what you can expect to happen, and a few things you need to remember about the process itself. Firstly, you should *always* arrive at an interview early - no excuses! Nothing shows you are disinterested in a job more than being late to an interview. It makes a bad first impression that is difficult to undo. Remember, you never get a second chance to make a good first impression. As I explain in the following chapter on preparation, plan to arrive 20 minutes before the interview.

If you don't already have specific instructions, you'll want to walk up to the first person you see. Usually this will be a receptionist or customer service person. "Hi, I'm here for an interview at 2:00 with Tom." It's okay if you don't know or don't remember the name of the person you'll be meeting for the interview. Some larger companies may also have you sign in on a visitor sheet and give you a visitor badge. They will then direct you where to go next.

You'll then meet the interviewer and be led to the interview location. Interviews are usually held in a closed room at the place of employment, such as an office or conference room, where you sit across from your interviewer. The table or desk between you creates a physical barrier or "safe zone" for both parties. It's also a way to keep things professional.

Most commonly, there will be one or two people interviewing you, although there can, in some cases, be anywhere from five to seven people, depending on the job. As one-on-one, face-to-face interviews are most common, we'll focus there for now, but later in the book we'll take a look at some other kinds of interviews and how they differ. Regardless, the number of interviewers or type of interview generally will not change what you need to do to be prepared.

After a friendly greeting, an exchange of names, and a firm handshake, the interviewer begins with some pleasantries. "How are you doing?" Tom asks. "Did you have any trouble finding the place?" He may also make some idle small talk, conversing about the weather as a means to calm nerves and transition into the more formal portion of the interview.

Sometimes, the interviewer will give you a quick overview of what to expect. "I've got some questions for you, and if you're not sure about something, just ask. I'll talk about some of the benefits, and then we'll allow time for your questions. We'll be together for about 45 minutes." If your interviewer doesn't say any of this, you can still assume that this will be the general format.

The interviewer will then begin to ask you a variety of questions about yourself, your previous work or school, and some probing questions, all of which we will cover in greater detail in the coming sections. Remember that it's okay at any time to say, "Would you repeat the question, please?" or, if you're not sure how to respond, you can say, "Can we come back to that?" You can also ask for clarification if you aren't sure you understand what's being asked. Remember that this isn't an interrogation! It's simply a conversation.

Once the interviewer is done with questions, you can ask your own questions, which we will also learn to prepare in advance later in this book. The interviewer will then close the interview by telling you about the next step in the process. "Well, we have some more candidates to interview, and we'll get back to you." You may also hear, "We'll keep in touch," or "We'll let you know by Friday." Don't over-think or read too much into these responses. Thank them for their time, and tell them you enjoyed meeting them.

And that's really all there is to the process. It's fairly straight-forward and isn't likely to vary wildly beyond that. The real keys to a successful interview are preparation and an understanding of what the interviewer is looking for. In the next chapter, you'll learn how to prepare, including how to develop natural responses to questions you may be asked, based on your own experience. These responses will satisfy them and set you up for a successful interview experience.

Chapter 4.
How Do I Prepare?

"My advice regarding interviewing can be summarized in one thought: practice. Practice with your spouse, your roommate, your mom. Practice with a career coach. Practice a lot. The more you practice, the more confident you will feel and the better answers you will be prepared to give."

- Jan Mead, Career & Job Search Coach

Years ago, I was interviewing for an x-ray tech position at a community hospital. At the start of the interview, the hiring manager asked, "Tell me about yourself." I answered, keeping my response brief. She then asked me if I had any questions about the job. I had a few. Then, after an awkward moment of silence, she said, "Well, if you don't have any additional questions, then that's really all there is for us to do." That was the entire interview! She had no questions for me whatsoever. It lasted...maybe 12 minutes total? Suffice it to say it was a very bizarre, one-sided interview experience.

A colleague once told me about an interview he had. He played basketball in college on a scholarship, and the hiring manager interviewing him was a big college basketball fan. When he saw that, he lit up and started talking about it. In total, out of the entire 45 minute interview, the interviewer spent 40 minutes talking about basketball. In the last five minutes, he said, "Well, I guess I should ask you some questions about whether or not you can do the job..." In the end, my colleague didn't feel that he got a chance to talk about his work accomplishments.

It may come as a surprise to realize that, in many cases, interviewing is not something the interviewer commonly does. As with the hiring manager for the x-ray tech position above, it may be uncomfortable for them and make them feel out of their element just as much as it does for you. Many times, they aren't even prepared for the interview. Other times, they can become distracted, such as the interviewer in the basketball story.

So here's where you'll really begin to shine - your preparation will keep them on-track, whether they are prepared or not. Even if they *are* prepared, how much better for you, then, that you are, too? The whole process can be stressful for some interviewers. The better prepared you are, the more you help put yourself *and* them at ease as well. This makes for a smoother and more successful interview process for both parties. Ironically, you'll also find that your responses in the interview will *seem* more spontaneous, even though you prepared for them. Interviewers like that. By being prepared, you have an immediate advantage.

WHERE DO I START?

Once you know when your interview will take place, you can start to get ready for it, both mentally and through some pre-work. You can begin by printing out the job description you applied for and comparing it side-by-side with your own list of qualifications. Which qualifications do you feel you meet? Which ones do you feel you don't?

Feel free to make some notes on the job description, and start to think about what questions you have about it. Are there some qualifications that you're not sure you meet? How important are those to them? What exactly do they mean by *that*? Write down at least 2 to 3 questions you have about the job that you want to ask the interviewer.

As my friend Jan Mead, Career and Job Search Coach, recommends to her clients, it's also a good idea to do a little research on the business online. Learn a little about their products or services, just enough to be familiar with what they do and where their headquarters are located. You may be asked what you know about the company, so it's good to have a general idea.

CAR

There's a single acronym I want you to remember that's crucial when preparing for any job interview - CAR. This stands for Challenge, Action, Results. A *Challenge* is a description of a task or situation that you faced. For example, you may have faced a difficult customer at a previous job. *Action* refers to what you did about it, so for example, maybe you talked the customer down. *Results* are the resolution to the situation - the customer was satisfied. The results are *very* important. These CAR examples will be invaluable in any job interview.

I remember a young woman I worked with a few years back. She was having difficulty landing a customer service role that she wanted. She told me they asked her questions such as, "What does customer service mean to you?" and "How do you define leadership?" She had been giving the textbook answers to these questions, but it just wasn't working. We worked together to formulate CAR examples from her own experience for each, and low and behold, she landed the next job she applied for. I ran into her a few months after she started the new job, and she said that they told her that her responses to their "stock" questions impressed them, because they had never heard anyone answer them like that before. This process is powerful, consistently works, and yet is still very uniquely you.

Well, how do I find CAR examples in my own experience? Think about the last 12 months of work or school. What projects did you work on? What ideas did you develop? What suggestions did you make for improvement? Did you catch any problems before they happened? Keep some of these examples fresh in your mind as you look at each part of the CAR process.

C - *What was the situation? Who was involved? What was the problem or opportunity?*

A - *What did you do? What did the team do? What did your supervisor do?*

R - *How did it turn out? What were the benefits to the team, company, or customer? What did you learn from the experience?*

This formula will become the guide for how you respond to all questions that involve your behaviors, your point-of-view, and hypothetical questions, using examples from your experience. Details are *essential*. Let's say you went to a doctor and found out you needed surgery. You ask him how many times he's performed the surgery, and he responds, "Oh, I don't know...a bunch of times." How confident does that make you feel? Ready to jump on the operating table for this guy? What if instead he said, "I've performed it 25 times, and it was a success each time." Details lend to credibility.

In preparation for your interview, write down seven to ten examples of tasks or situations you faced using CAR.

These don't have to be big challenges, either. Always try to keep the three parts down to roughly one or two sentences each. This will keep you from rambling on and on and remain focused on the main point. It may also prompt your interviewer to want to ask follow-up questions about your example, which makes them more engaged with you and what you've said. Interviewers want to be engaged with you in an interview. They want to know who you are. Stock answers tell them nothing. So in your next interview, when you're asked, "What does customer service mean to you?" you can give a *specific* example of what it means to you.

When I first started doing career counseling 20 years ago, I ran a job search support group on Thursday evenings. One of the people in the group told us he had been fired from his management job of 15 years because he had been drinking on the job. He admitted he had a problem and that his job loss motivated him to seek counseling. In the six months since his termination, he had been sober and wanted to get back to work. He had done several interviews already, but he always stumbled over the answer when he was asked why he was let go from his previous job. He was ashamed of what happened and didn't know how to get past it. We talked about it, and he found a way to discuss it honestly, without blame or guilt. The key was that he kept the answer short and solution-focused. He took responsibility for his actions, explained that he had gotten help since that time, and stressed that he was now committed to his work. He used a simple CAR approach as a concise answer, rather than trying to make excuses and blame situations on the spot. Within three weeks, he had another interview, answered the question with confidence, and got the job.

Like him, something to consider as you prepare for an interview is this: What is the one question you hope they won't ask you? If you can look at that question and develop an honest (and not blaming) response, you are prepared with your answer. Like the man above, reframe that question to ask yourself, "What was the Challenge? (had a drinking problem), What was the Action taken? (got help), What are the Results? (ready to go back to work, focused)." It may not come up, but it's better to be prepared than to be caught off-guard.

There was a 16-month gap in my employment at one time years ago. It was something that I knew would be difficult to talk about in an interview. I could easily have ended up rambling on and on about the details of the situation. When it was asked, though, I used the CAR structure to respond honestly and concisely, "[C] A family member had a serious illness. [A] It was a tough decision, but I chose to come home to take care of that family member. [R] Now, that situation has resolved, and I'm excited to get back to work!" Even difficult questions can be addressed honestly, if you use the CAR framework.

THE DAY APPROACHES

You've done some pre-work, developed some CAR examples, and prepared questions. The day of the interview is fast approaching. Time to get yourself ready. Once you know when it will take place, don't schedule anything else that day, like a doctor's appointment before-hand. An interview deserves your full attention. Confirm where it will be located and what you need to bring. You can do this either through mail, email, or a phone call - whichever way they've communicated with you so far is probably the best way for you to communicate back with them.

There are also some things you should do no later than the day before the interview. Trying to do these things *on* the day of the interview will cause unneeded stress or risk you being late to the interview. Determine what you'll wear. If you're not sure, check online and see what kind of business it is and what employees are shown wearing in photos. As a rule of thumb, plan to wear clothing that is either about the same level or one level higher than what they wear. So, if they wear a polo shirt and jeans, wear something similar, or even go up to business casual. Don't go underdressed.

The day before, get your car cleaned out and get it washed. This might seem unrelated, but it will make you feel better, because physical clutter can clutter your mind. And there's always a chance that, after your interview, they may walk you to your car. As you'll find out later in the book, your first impression actually starts when you arrive, and that includes your car.

Find out where you need to go, plan your route to get there, and decide where you'll plan to park. Getting lost on the way to an interview is the last thing you want to have happen! To ease any anxiety, if possible, drive to the location two days before, so you can estimate the time needed to get to the interview.

Plan to bring your notes with you to the interview, and plan to take some during it. Don't rely solely on your memory. The night before, set your alarm and double-check it. Finally, get plenty of sleep!

The day of the interview, make sure to start with good hygiene - don't come to the interview looking like you've just rolled out of bed. Allow an extra 15 minutes for travel time; you never know what kind of delays traffic might bring. Arrive 20 minutes early, sit in your car, and allow some time to mentally prepare yourself for the meeting. Briefly review your questions about the job and your CARs before going in. This will keep them fresh in your mind. Don't go over every single detail of your résumé and notes, though. Paraphrase the CARs you have. Spending too much time on this will confuse you or possibly overwhelm you. You're not taking a test! It's simply a conversation.

Despite all this preparation, there will always be nerves about new places, people, and wanting to do your best. Use the time in your car to mentally prepare by taking some of the pressure away. What I like to do is think of something funny to take the stress off. Maybe a funny video I saw, or something encouraging a family member said. You might want to quietly listen to some of your favorite music. Take a few deep breaths. Just do something to stop worrying for a few minutes. I will strongly suggest, however, that you *do not* check your email, texts, Facebook or anything like that. They will occupy your thoughts and distract you during an interview. Set aside any other tasks, projects, and communications you have until *after* the interview.

Until you finish the interview and leave, keep your focus on it and it alone.

As important as a job interview can be, remember to keep a little perspective, too. The outcome of the interview *does not* determine your worth as a human being. You might feel like you'll be judged, as many people do in any kind of new situation. Just remember that feelings aren't facts, and you're only imagining what you think others think of you; you don't actually know what they're thinking. Be discriminating in who you *allow* to judge you in your mind. It's a good thing to get feedback, but not everyone is qualified to give it. No matter what kinds of judgment you may have felt in the past, no one is going into the interview but you - no negative bosses or critical relatives - just you. Every new encounter is a fresh start.

Remind yourself that this isn't a fight or a competition; it's simply a meeting. You and the interviewer are coming together to talk about a common interest - your needs and their needs. Resist the idea that interviewing is a strategic duel or that you have to "trick" them into giving you what you want, using some kind of sales technique. Some questionable online sources will tell you to push for a decision or job offer, using phrases that are unnatural to you and sound rehearsed. How does it feel when you are pushed for a sale by someone else? Don't do that! It's insulting to the other person, it's a turn-off, and it will fail. It will confuse the interviewer, and a confused mind says "no."

Finally, before you go in for your interview, turn your cell phone off! No exceptions! Do not check it during the interview. And NO GUM! Ten minutes before your interview, go in and check in with reception or customer service. I recommend 10 minutes because you want to arrive early, but any earlier can be kind of awkward.

A PERSONAL NOTE FROM ME ABOUT YOUR JOB SEARCH

I know that the process of looking for a job and being interviewed is time-consuming, stressful, and often quite discouraging. During these times, turn to someone supportive that will encourage you along the way. Seek out a job search support group, a good friend or a professional coach. While you can always turn to a family member, these people outside your family care about you as a person but are removed enough from you that they can be objective. Don't just bottle it up. During a critical time in my career, Chris Wallace, an Executive Coach and Career Management Consultant, encouraged me to look to those people who will be your confidants. Don't do life alone.

PREPARATION CHECKLIST

- Research the company or organization so that you can answer the question, "What do you know about our company?"
- Compare the job description, line by line, with your skills and experience
- Write and review at least six CARs of things you've done within the last five years
- Create a written list of questions to ask the interviewers, including clarifying questions about the job requirements and other questions (see Chapter 8)
- Copy of the job description
- Practice getting to the company and seeing where you should park and enter the building. Do this at least two days in advance.
- Clear your schedule for the day of the interview so that you have nothing else on your mind that day
- Plan your clothes for the interview, cleaned and ready the night before
- Make sure your car is clean on the inside and the outside – you never know if they'll walk you to your car!
- Get a good night's sleep
- Arrive at the location so that you can walk into the building with at least 10 minutes to spare before the interview appointment time
- Turn off your cell phone; not vibrate mode – off!

Chapter 5. How To Present Yourself - The Whole Picture

"The more you like yourself, the less you are like anyone else, which makes you unique." - Walt Disney

How you present yourself is immensely important. Take this story for example.

A colleague and I once interviewed a guy who came on *very* strong. He was loud. He was obnoxious. He interrupted. He acted far too familiar with us, as if we were all buddies. "You know, I just *love* the company's mission statement, don't you? Isn't it just *awesome*?!" I felt like I was being sold a vacation time share! He didn't listen to us at all and just kept pushing by asking, "So, how am I doing so far? How do I compare to your other applicants?" After the interview, he called the main switchboard, got our phone numbers, and called each of us on the interviewing team with the same questions above. This was completely against what we had told him, which was that *we* would contact *him*. The whole experience was uncomfortably aggressive, and this only confirmed for us that we were not interested in him.

Remember how I said that you'll come across advice online to push and sell yourself? This guy was a prime example of that. He had no humility, didn't listen to us, tried to force himself on us, and really crossed a line by trying to contact us separately to push for a review. He may have been a nice guy, but we'd never know that because of the way he presented himself. Interviewers are looking for teachability, not to be overrun. Is it any surprise that we didn't want to work with him? Yes, you want to sell yourself in the interview, but you don't want to come across like a used car salesman. The best way to sell yourself is to *be yourself.*

THE UNWRITTEN RULES

Of course, in any professional situation, there will be some unspoken social expectations and things you should never do that you need to be aware of. Here are some to consider.

BE PROFESSIONAL, NO MATTER WHAT

Once, when I was working as a Human Resources Generalist, I'd scheduled a face-to-face interview with a candidate for a coordinator position. Two minutes before the scheduled time, the candidate walked into the office with her two small kids in tow. "I almost didn't make it. My babysitter canceled at the last minute, and I couldn't get a replacement. Can you get someone to watch my kids while I interview?" Needless to say, we were not equipped nor prepared to babysit in the office. I did offer to reschedule the appointment, to which she responded, "I don't have time to reschedule now. I'm here now. Can't you just watch my kids?"

What do you think of that situation? Did she act professionally? How could she have avoided that predicament?

. . . .

SOCIAL RULES FOR INTERVIEWING

. . . .

Limit your comments about the place or what you see.

Even well-intended comments can go awry. I made this mistake many years ago while interviewing for a professional position. I noticed a picture of a woman on the interviewer's desk. I said, "Oh, is that your wife?"

"No, actually it's my mother." *Awkward...*

Use professional language and avoid inappropriate humor.

In an attempt to get comfortable with the interviewer(s), some people will use humor to break the ice. Jokes have their place; their place is not in the interview. The same goes for sarcasm. It may get you a laugh, but it won't score points with the interviewers.

Also, not everyone reacts positively to swearing, so keep your language PG.

Avoid language or expressions that assume the other person knows what you're talking about.

We were interviewing a man for a director's position. He was actually doing fairly well with the interview until we asked him what he liked about working for his current supervisor. He told us she was okay, except for her being *emotional*. His words were, "You know how women are." I half-expected a wink and a nudge to follow. This type of familiarity and sexism is inappropriate for the interview, not to mention for the workplace!

It's an interview, not a counseling session.

Most all of us have had unpleasant experiences at work, ranging from crappy supervisors to irritating co-workers. I feel your pain and empathize. Now, here's my point. Don't bring that up in the interview. It doesn't matter if you were right and they were wrong. *Don't bring that up in the interview.* How about a "personality conflict" at work? *Don't bring that up in an interview.* I can't stress this enough. I'm the kind of person who others tend to see as empathetic and a good listener. They get comfortable with me when I'm interviewing them and they start unloading on me. You may gain my sympathy, but you don't gain my vote for proceeding in the selection process. Save the need for expressing your pain in an appropriate way and with the appropriate persons, not in an interview.

Avoid the "Creeper" effect.

I like to research the company and the people I'm interviewing with prior to the interview. In fact, I recommend that you do company research before your appointment. However, you don't need to share everything you discover online with the interviewers. One time, when I was in a series interview, and a finalist for a position, I was meeting with the Human Resources Director. There was a lull in the conversation, and I wanted to ease the discomfort of the quiet. "I noticed on your LinkedIn profile that you used to work in California. I'm originally from California." Her eyes went wide, and she politely confirmed this, going on to the next question. I knew I blew it. I had crossed the line from candidate to creeper. And yes, you guessed it, I didn't get a call back.

Never, never, never check your cell phone at any time during the interview process.

Your focus is on the appointment. Text messages, Facebook updates, or the latest tweets can wait until you're done and off the premises. I saw this happen in an interview that we were conducting once. Right in the middle of the interview, the candidate took a phone call. "I'll have to call you back," he said to the person on the other end of the phone. This interruption made it clear that he wasn't that focused in the interview.

HONESTY IS NOT JUST THE BEST POLICY, IT'S THE ONLY POLICY

I once answered an ad for a training position. Among the many job requirements, the ad listed "experience with eLearning course development." At that time, I had none. So in my cover letter I said that I didn't have experience with that. During a panel interview (where three people interviewed me at once), one of the interviewers asked why I put that in my cover letter.

"Because it's true, I don't have any experience with that."

"We just wondered why you mentioned it at all."

"I put that in there because I didn't know how important that item is to you. If it isn't that important, then at least you know I don't have experience. If it is important to you, then you need to know that as well."

I got the job. Later, that interviewer told me that my honesty in that answer really impressed them.

I couldn't tell from the job description whether or not experience with that was really important to them. The fact that they listed experience with that in the job description was a signal to me that I needed to respond to it. Think of the job requirements as questions rather than statements. So, for the example above, the requirement read, "Experience with e-Learning." I read it as, "What is my experience with e-Learning?" Converting these statements into questions to ask yourself will frame them up for you to prepare your honest answer.

EVERYTHING YOU DO OR SAY IS BEING WATCHED

This isn't meant to scare you, but understand that your interview actually starts the moment you arrive at the location to the moment you leave. Be aware of how you present yourself at all times during the process. What you do before and after an interview is just as important as during the interview.

Case in point: While I was working at a university, we once interviewed a woman for a professional position. The interview was okay overall. After the interview, as we talked, we watched her leave the building, go outside, and start picking leaves off the trees in front of the building! We put that in our interview notes. Later that day, several people from other offices told us that she had spent her time before the interview walking into their departments and looking around. When they asked her if they could help her, she just said she "wanted to get a feel for the place." She crossed a line in social etiquette, disturbing others in their work when it wasn't her place to be doing that. She was picking leaves when all she needed to do was leave.

Another time, not long ago, I interviewed a man for a custodial position. At the conclusion of the interview, I walked him to the elevator and thanked him for coming in. He asked me, "Can you give me some money for a cab ride? I didn't bring enough with me." Seriously? In my mind, he just went from a candidate to a pan handler on the street. It made me feel very uncomfortable. In another situation, I would probably help him out, but given that we just interviewed, it was very out of line. Don't put your interviewer on the spot.

IT'S NOT "WHAT THEY CAN DO FOR YOU" - - IT'S "WHAT YOU CAN DO FOR THEM"

Think about the interview from the company's perspective for a moment. They have a problem, and they're hoping that you'll be able to solve that problem and that you'll be a good fit for the team. In the same way, you're hoping you can solve their problem and that you will fit in with the team. Too often I've heard candidates respond to the question, "What are you looking for in an ideal position?" with "A place where I can build my skills and grow in my career; a company that will provide me with opportunities for advancement; an organization that provides good pay and benefits; lifelong employment," and the list goes on. These aren't bad in and of themselves; they're probably true for most people.

My point is that each of these responses is focused on what the company can do for you. It's very self-serving and comes across that you really aren't concerned about the company's needs - only your own. When you are sitting on the other side of the interviewing table, on the side of the company, you want to know what the person can do for the company. Can you solve our problem? Do you fit with the team? A better way to frame up the answer to the question, "What are you looking for in an ideal position?" is to talk about how you can use your talent, strengths, skills, and abilities to add value to the organization by solving their problems and being a contributing member of the team.

CHAPTER 6.
WHAT QUESTIONS
MIGHT THEY ASK ME?

There are five primary types of questions you will be asked during a job interview. Firstly, there are closed-ended ones, like, "Do you have experience with Microsoft Excel?" or "How many years experience do you have in this field?" These are straight-forward, factual questions answered with a yes, no, or with a number. Secondly, there are more open-ended questions, like "What do you like most about your type of work?" or "Tell me about yourself." The interviewer is asking these two types of questions because they want to know more details about you.

The other three types are behavior-based questions, hypothetical questions, and point-of-view questions. You'll find that these, along with some open-ended, are the types of questions where CAR comes into play. Remember that CAR stands for Challenge, Action, Results.

Before we explore those other types, let's take a look at common open-ended questions and how you can best respond to them.

COMMON OPEN-ENDED QUESTIONS

Some common examples are examined below. With each of these, consider how you might respond before you go into the interview.

"Tell me about yourself."

Research from a variety of sources confirms that this is the most frequently asked question during the interview.

Where do I start? you may be thinking. For some, it's difficult to sum up who you are or what makes you...you. To answer this question, prepare a brief two to three minute summary of your work experience in advance. Again, start with what you are currently doing and summarize the last five to ten years of your work history. Keeping your response to less than three minutes forces you to keep from rambling and keeps the interview going at an appropriate pace. Write it out and practice it aloud. Also, practice it in front of someone you trust who will give you honest feedback. The best time to practice anything is before you get to the interview, not *at* the interview. I once suffered through someone's entire life story, starting off with, "Well, I was born on a farm in Iowa. I went to school and played sports..." *Arghh!*

"Why did you leave your last job?" or *"Why do you want to make a change right now?"*

This is not meant to be a trick question. The interviewer is trying to get a sense of what happened that made you leave or made you want to leave. Was it something you decided or something your employer decided? In either case, do not, I repeat, *do not* talk badly about your former employer. Answer honestly and sincerely, and keep your answer brief, to-the-point, and positive.

Think about it this way: Suppose you order a meal at a restaurant, it arrives late and is cold. Would you prefer to hear long-winded excuses and explanations of how the cook did *such and such*, and how someone was late to their shift, etc., or would you rather hear an apology and an offer asking, "What can we do to make this up to you?" One is talking about the *problem*, the other is talking about the *solution*. Talk about the solution. If you made a mistake and got fired, be honest and tell them that, as well as what you learned from the experience. Now is not the time to defend your ego. Remember, interviewers are people who have probably gone through similar ups and downs in their careers. They want to understand why you left or want to leave.

They may also ask, "What did you like most, and what did you like least?" Have a 3-to-1 ratio of 3 things you liked and 1 you didn't like. You can be honest, but you don't want to give an overly negative impression.

"Do you consider yourself a self-starter?" and *"Are you a team player?"*

Now consider, who would actually answer "No" to that question? Nevertheless, give a CAR example for these kinds of questions and perhaps an example of how you worked with a team in the past.

"What are your strengths?"

I find this question intriguing because strengths means different things to different people. What I do is talk about my strengths as other people see them. So as an example, I've said, "According to my last supervisor, one of my strengths is being able to anticipate customer needs and provide creative solutions. Would you like an example?" I ask the interviewer if he or she would like an example so that can open the door to a CAR related to the strength. If they do want an example, keep it short.

"What are your weaknesses?"

Please take the time to really think this one through. If you start talking about your skill gaps that are unrelated to the job you are applying for, you will confuse the interviewers. Only talk about skill gaps that relate directly to the job and talk about how you intend to address that gap. For example, I interviewed someone for a position who responded, "Although I have experience in this type of job, I've never worked in this industry before. I've thought a lot about that, and I want to spend time learning the industry and the business, if I get hired." I liked that response because it was honest and solution-focused.

"Why do you want to work here?" or *"What about this job appeals to you?"*

Honestly talk about how you think your strengths and abilities can help solve their problems. Avoid comments about the great pay and benefits you've heard about. The interviewers don't want to hear about that. Keep your focus on the fit between you and their needs.

"I notice you've had several jobs in the last ten years. Can you talk about that?"

It's becoming less and less common for a person to work for the same company for 30 years and then retire, as it seemed to be in my parents' generation. The business world has changed. Recent studies have shown that you will change jobs to a different company an average of seven times in your lifetime.

For years, I was embarrassed that I had moved around to different companies, usually spending four or five years at each. A good friend, Tim Link, Executive Coach, helped me to see that these different jobs were not a reason to feel bad at all. In fact, they have given me a very rich variety of experiences from which to draw. I'll always be thankful to Tim for helping me reframe my experience.

So if you have had several previous employers and are asked this question, be honest and tell them why you moved around. Focus on the positive reasons why you made the changes you did. Stay away from putting down your previous employers.

"Why should we hire you?"

The interviewer is asking you to help them make the connection between what you bring to the job and their needs. This question usually occurs towards the end of the interview. The best way to answer is to summarize the top three things they need for the position and your qualifications for each of those needs. Narrowing in on the top three needs or problems shows that you were listening during the interview and that you are making the connection between their needs and your ability to meet those needs.

BEHAVIOR-BASED QUESTIONS

Behavior-based questions may begin, "Tell me about a time when you..." or "Give me an example of..." The interviewer is asking these because *past behavior predicts future performance*. In other words, how you've dealt with things in the past gives them a preview of how you might handle things in this job. The power is in the details, so as usual, don't give generalized answers. If it's generalized, it's not believable. Here are some examples of these questions: "Give me an example of a communication breakdown you had with a co-worker or other person at work." "Tell me about a time when you had to act, and you didn't have all the information you needed." We'll tackle these in the upcoming Examples section.

. . . .

HYPOTHETICAL QUESTIONS

. . . .

Hypothetical questions are similar, but in this case, an interviewer wants to know how you *would* handle something if given the job. "If *such* and *such* happened, what would you do?" Always answer these hypothetical questions with CAR examples from your experience that are similar to the proposed situation.

. . . .

POINT-OF-VIEW QUESTIONS

. . . .

Point-of-view questions differ from hypothetical questions in that they are trying to determine your perspective on something. "What does customer service mean to you?" "What's the most important thing for a successful team?" "What kind of management style do you prefer to work under?" These questions are trying to find out more about *how* you work.

I was being interviewed for a management position with a university several years ago. A person on the interview team asked me, "How do you define leadership?" I recounted a CAR from my past that highlighted what I had done, reflecting personal leadership. The interviewer then asked me more questions about that situation, and it turned into a productive conversation about leadership philosophy and practice. The point I'm making here is that if I had given a generic textbook answer, such as, "I believe that the safest ship in a storm is leadership," or something similar, it may not have led to a conversation about leadership. Providing a real-life CAR was the starting point for a further conversation relevant to the job, which allowed us to connect by learning from each other.

. . . .

REGARDING SALARY

. . . .

"What are your expectations for pay?"

If you're interviewing for an entry-level position, they will likely just tell you. For most other positions, it depends on how early in the interview they ask it. If they ask very early on, something I would say is, *"If it's a good fit between what you need and what I bring, then I'm sure we can work something out."* You have to build up value in their eyes throughout the interview before you talk about pay. If a number is presented too early, you will be compared to that number throughout the interview, rather than being assessed solely on your own merits. The way you establish value is through your CARs. If asked later, near the end of the interview, respond with, *"What's your range for the position?"* or *"What is your offer?"* They will either come back with a range or specific number, or they will redirect the question back to you.

If they redirect by saying, "We really need to know what your expectations are," then you can respond with something along the lines of, *"Based on my understanding of the job and how my skills and abilities fit what you're looking for, I would need $_____."* Once you say the number, keep quiet and say nothing else. If you keep talking, you're over-selling, and they need time to think about what you've proposed. Also, excess talking indicates that you aren't confident in that number yourself. The number you propose will have to come from some research beforehand - you can look online for what salary ranges are typical for that kind of position, and sometimes the company will post it on their website. You can also talk to others to find out what a position like the one you're interested in might pay.

WHAT'S BEHIND THE QUESTIONS?

Most interview questions have an underlying question behind them. For example, a behavior-based question, such as, "Tell me about a time when you found an error in your work, and how did you handle it?" is not so much about the error but about personal integrity. So the question behind this question is, "Do you have personal integrity?" What's behind a point-of-view question is similar. "What do you like most about your current supervisor?" is really asking, "Will your expectations and my supervisory style be a match or be a problem?"

Although it helps to know that there is a question behind the question, it's important not to dwell on that. In the interview, I stress the importance of being in the moment. If you are frantically trying to figure out what they're "really asking" with each question, you are not in the moment, and your focus is on guessing instead of answering. I cannot stress enough – *focus on answering the question and resist the temptation to analyze.*

An additional tip I recommend is to occasionally confirm after CAR responses by asking, "Does that answer your question?" or "Is that what you were looking for?" This question looks for confirmation from them, and it will allow them to course-correct you, if needed. It also shows that you are engaged in the discussion and want to make a good impression. Don't do this for *every* question; instead, perhaps use it for every several questions, just so it doesn't feel redundant.

EXAMPLES

Below are some behavior-based questions with a few sample responses to get you started. Use these to begin to craft your own answers and practice responding.

1. Tell me about a mistake you made on the job and what you learned from it.

- **Weak answer:**

  "I don't make any mistakes." This is a real answer I've received from one of the people I've told you about. This is weak because it doesn't give any details, and it's arrogant.

- **Strong answer:**

  (Challenge) "We were doing audits, and I found an error I made on the report I'd already sent to a manager in a different department."

  (Action) "I called the manager and told her what the mistake I made was, apologized, and told her what I could do to make up for the mistake."

  (Results) "She thanked me for my honesty and told me that my solution would be acceptable; I also let my supervisor know what had happened. I learned that I'd rather be honest than try to cover up and protect my pride."

2. Give me an example of a communication breakdown you had with a co-worker or other person at work.

- **Weak answer:**

  "Generally, I try to get along with everyone. That's what makes for good teamwork, right?" This again is a general statement which doesn't tell the interviewers anything about how the candidate handles conflict or miscommunication at work.

- **Strong answer:**

  (Challenge) "There was a time when I was working with a colleague on a project that had a pretty tight deadline. The breakdown in communication came because we got so busy focusing on our own part of the project, we neglected to keep each other informed of our respective progress. This resulted in some duplication of effort and we both found ourselves a bit frustrated about that."

  (Action) "Once we both realized what we were doing, or more accurately not doing, we scheduled some quick daily meetings to go over our individual progress on the project."

  (Results) "After we started meeting on a daily basis, we discovered that we could also help each other by continuing to review our progress. In the end, we finished on time and had a good laugh!"

3. Tell me about a time when you had to act, and you didn't have all the information you needed.

- **Weak answer**:

  "I would never do that. That could lead to mistakes, and any business person knows that mistakes are costly. I always make sure I have the information I need, and if I don't, I go get it." No details; not helpful.

- **Strong answer**:

  (Challenge) "This has to with a customer that needed something right away. I needed to get approval from my supervisor in order to proceed, but, unfortunately, my supervisor was away, and I couldn't reach him. I know how it feels, as a customer, to need something and to get put off because the person I'm talking to doesn't have the authority to make the decision."

  (Action) "So I thought about it and decided to meet the customer's request."

  (Results) "The customer was very pleased and thanked me. When my supervisor returned, I told him about the situation and what I had done. He said that I did the right thing. That made me feel good, since I wasn't really sure at the time."

PRACTICE

Now that you've seen some examples, try developing your own CAR responses for these questions:

1. Tell me about a mistake you made on the job and what you learned from it.

2. Give me an example of a communication breakdown you had with a co-worker or other person at work.

3. Tell me about a time when you had to act, and you didn't have all the information you needed.

4. Tell me about a time when you took the initiative to act, even though you weren't told to do so.

5. Give me a specific example of when you felt you acted in the best interest of a customer.

6. Tell me about a time when you disagreed with your supervisor. How did you handle it?

7. Give me an example of an instance when you took the time to help another co-worker.

8. Tell me about a recent project you worked on. How did you manage your time and priorities?

9. Give me an example of a time when you came up with an idea or a suggestion for improvement.

10. There's stress in every job. Tell me about a time you were under stress and how you handled it.

Chapter 7. Keeping Focus

"Impossible to see, the future is." - Yoda

Stay in the moment! For some people, it's hard not to want to analyze every little detail going on around them in the interview, as you pick up on some non-verbal cues around you. One thing you might notice is that it's very likely your interviewer hasn't really looked over your résumé until just then. This is common. Again, remember that this process is not normally what the interviewer does. Don't take it personally. It doesn't mean they aren't interested; they probably just haven't had extra time to look it over.

With all these questions and new information coming your way, it's easy to start to let your mind wander to all sorts of possibilities. You may think you know what direction the conversation is leading towards. However, again, it is essential to be in the moment. Don't try to anticipate what might be coming next. It's hard not to want to jump ahead in your mind to what the next question might be (even as they are still on the current one) or to beat yourself up for feeling like you answered a question poorly. As difficult as it may sound, try to put your emotions aside.

As I've said before, don't look *too* hard for what hidden meaning might be behind what's being said. *Why did he ask that? What's he really implying about me?* Over-thinking will just make you nervous. Stop trying to figure out what they're really asking. Just answer the questions as they come. Second guessing will put you in second place!

You also can't be anticipating the outcome of the interview while you're in the interview. This mistake can screw everything up. If you're thinking about the outcome, it pulls you away from the moment, you aren't genuine, and they will pick up on that. Keep in mind that the interviewer may also be struggling being in the moment, as no doubt, interviewing you is one thing on a much longer list of things for them to do that day. Do not project into the future, despite whatever tempting benefits are being dangled in front of you. You'll miss warning signs, like a need that hasn't been expressed, or signs of poor management. Just let the process unfold naturally, and stay in the present moment.

HOW I STAY IN THE MOMENT

Prepare, but don't anticipate. Preparation is helpful; anticipation is not. Don't spend all your energy worrying about the outcome, including *while* you're interviewing. Take things one step at a time. Your focus should always be on the interview, not beyond that. There are many ways to stay in the moment, and there's no one right answer for everyone. Here are some that I use when I'm in an interview.

REMEMBER - I remind myself - *"It's just a conversation."* Remember that you're not on trial. They aren't judging you as a human being; they are just trying to determine if you are a good fit for what they need.

REASSURE - I remind myself of where I am (in this job interview), and that I was able to get here. Try reminding yourself, *"I'm in the interview now, I've made it this far, and that's something to be proud of."*

RELAX - I take a few deep breaths and smile. Take the pressure off yourself. Ultimately, you're only responsible for what you say and do. You're not responsible for how they might interpret that. *"The only thing I can control in this situation is myself."*

Chapter 8.
Questions For You To Ask Them

Always have your questions ready. In addition to questions you might have regarding the job description, it's helpful to prepare some probing questions for them that give you an idea of what they are really looking for.

There was an academic account position open once, I applied for it, and landed an interview. There were four people sitting at a table opposite me this time. After about 40 minutes, they asked me if I had any questions. "What are the top three qualities you're looking for in the ideal candidate?" I asked. "Well, someone with lots of sales experience is top of our list." This was insightful, since I didn't have a lot of sales experience. It certainly was not made clear on the job description, either. Without asking the question, I wouldn't have known what really mattered to them. In turn, it may have also helped them clarify what was really important. The net result is that I didn't get the job, and I'm glad I didn't. It wasn't a right fit for either of us.

A job might look great on the outside, but you could be spending *a lot* of your time there, so it's best to get a feel for things as early in the hiring process as the interview with some probing questions. Here are my top three favorite questions:

1. *"What are the qualities you're looking for in the ideal candidate?"*

With this question, you're essentially asking them to confirm that what you've been presenting during the interview aligns with what they are looking for.

2. *"What does success look like for this job?"*

This question will get the interviewer to tell you what's really important to them.

3. *"What's the most important thing I would start working on first?"*

This gives you a preview of what you'd expect, should you start working for this employer, and what their expectations will be.

Beyond these kinds of questions, keep them technically focused on the job itself. It's also okay to ask what the next step in the process will be.

One question you should *never* ask is, "How do I compare to your other candidates?" This kind of question puts them on the spot in a way that is not appropriate. The question makes the interviewer have to make a sudden snap decision about you when they really need time to reflect on the whole interview. It's also very presumptuous and somewhat confrontive to try to get inside information about competition, which suddenly twists the dynamics of the people in the interview. Besides, even if they did answer, they're not going to be completely honest anyway, in the same way not everyone will complain about bad food when a server asks, "How was your meal?" at a restaurant. Some prefer to kindly lie, saying, "It was fine," and then no longer do business with them.

In general, I recommend that you don't even think about competition for a job. Aside from rare group interviews, there's no one in the room but you and the interviewer(s). Just focus on presenting yourself, as that's the only person you *can* control.

PRACTICE

Below are some sample questions you can ask an interviewer:

1. What are the top three qualities you're looking for in the ideal candidate?

2. What are the top priorities for the position?

3. What are the top priorities for the organization or group?

4. How do you measure success for this position?

5. What resources do I have to help me get started?

6. How will I know if I'm doing a good job of meeting your expectations?

7. What does success look like for this role?

CHAPTER 9.
OTHER TYPES OF INTERVIEWS

There are plenty of variations on job interviews, but in general, the process remains the same. Here are some of the more common variations you might come across:

PHONE SCREEN INTERVIEWS

These are interviews held over the phone and are very common. Usually, they serve as a screening interview done with a Human Resources person or recruiter before you continue to an in-person interview. Preparation remains the same. An important thing to remember to do is to get dressed up as if you were actually going to a face-to-face interview. This puts you in the mental frame of mind you would have in a face-to-face interview.

Find a quiet, private place where you can conduct the interview, sitting down, and will be undisturbed. Take notes. Do NOT use your speaker phone; you want to have a clear connection. Do not try to multitask and work on anything else; give it your undivided attention. These interviews are typically shorter in length, so expect 15 to 30 minutes.

Now, one of my favorite true stories - I kid you not, this actually happened. I was the recruiter for a university. I set up a phone interview with a candidate for a managerial position in maintenance. At the scheduled time, I called him, and we began our interview. It started out fine, but about five minutes in, he asked me, "Can you hold for a moment?" "Sure." This is what I heard, slightly muffled because he was holding his hand over the phone. "Yeah,...uhh...I'll have a number three value meal with a large iced tea..." I couldn't believe it! He was actually ordering fast food *while* interviewing! When he got back on the line, I proceeded to get through the interview as quickly as possible. Unsurprisingly, he did not move forward in the selection process. But I'm sure he enjoyed that cheeseburger... As you can see, preparing for a phone interview and making sure you are in a private place, without distractions, is a make-or-break factor.

VIDEO CALL INTERVIEWS

These are similar to the Phone Screen Interviews above. So again, do all the preparation you would for a face-to-face. In addition, be aware of what that person will see behind you wherever you're sitting, and make any necessary changes. Make sure you have a good internet connection and that you can hear each other clearly. Dress nicely, and act as you would in a face-to-face conversation - that's essentially what's happening, only digitally.

SERIES INTERVIEWS

In a series, you'll meet face-to-face with one person, then another, and so on. They typically last around 30 minutes to an hour each, one after another with brief breaks in between. It can feel a bit like a marathon. It's best to plan nothing else that day, if you can. Drink water, and ask for water *only*. Don't drink anything else in case it spills. It's also one less thing to have to manage if you're not trying to juggle your notes *and* a coffee mug. Note-taking is very helpful in a series interview, and I recommend taking a lot of notes, as it's hard to keep track of who's who otherwise. It's absolutely okay to use the same CARs from one interviewer to the next. They will compare their notes, and it shows consistency.

LUNCH INTERVIEWS

Commonly, these will be one-on-one or two-on-one. They are essentially the same as a face-to-face interview, only less formal. The employer always pays for the meal. I strongly recommend you order something simple to eat like a sandwich or some soup. Avoid foods that are messy or noisy. Sorry, fettuccini alfredo and spaghetti are out! Do not order a big meal, and do not order dessert. Take smaller bites and eat slower; you might be asked questions while you're in the middle of a bite. Answering questions with a mouth full of food isn't exactly appealing. You may not be able to eat your whole meal, or you may still be hungry, but that's okay. It's not about the lunch, it's about the interview. You can always get something else afterwards.

PANEL INTERVIEWS

These face-to-face interviews will have two to five people interviewing you, one at a time. It may feel a little more intimidating to feel outnumbered. Despite this, preparation is still the same as a regular face-to-face interview. The only major difference is that you'll get questions from several different people and follow-up questions from a different person than the one who asked the initial question.

My primary tip in this situation is this: When one person asks you a question, as you begin your answer, speak to the person who asked the question; then, as you continue to answer, start looking at the other people on the panel. This makes everyone feel included in the answer, not just the one who asked. It won't seem like you're having a private conversation with one person, while the others are just present to watch. This is very effective in engaging everyone in the room.

GROUP INTERVIEWS

These are more common for entry-level positions, such as in retail. It's rare to encounter a group interview at a professional level, but it can happen. In a group interview, you and several other candidates will interview at the same time in the same room. The interviewer commonly asks a question and each candidate responds in turn. If the opportunity presents itself, you can provide a short CAR example.

Don't interrupt other candidates. Limit your socializing with the other candidates, as it can distract. You aren't there to make new friends, you're there to interview. As much as you can, focus on the interviewer(s) and answering their questions. Don't focus on comparing yourself to the other candidates and their responses. Try to stay in the moment. It's not easy, and not ideal, but it is doable.

Chapter 10. It's Over, So What Happens Next?

"There are two kinds of worries - those you can do something about and those you can't. Don't spend any time on the latter."
- Duke Ellington

You've made it through the interview! Congratulations! Now go celebrate; treat yourself to something you enjoy. Even with preparation, interviewing can be stressful, so give your mind and body a rest.

It's easy to want to replay everything that happened in your head, and analyze every little thing that was said or left unsaid. Make a deal with yourself that you won't review what happened for 24 hours. This gives you time to let your emotions return to normal before thinking about it. Dwelling on it will cause you to second-guess *everything*.

If the interviewer told you that they'd let you know by a certain day, and it passes by, it's okay to call or email them. Say something like, "Hi, it's _____, just following up. I was just wondering where we are in the selection process. I'm looking forward to hearing from you. Have a good day."

POSSIBLE OUTCOMES

So what happens next? Well, there are three possibilities:

YOU DON'T HEAR BACK FROM THEM

You can try contacting them twice, as I suggested above, but after that you need to let it go. In an ideal world, everyone would be told whether they got the job or not, but it doesn't always happen that way. From my own experience, it can be very frustrating to hear some good feedback and "We'll get back to you" only to wait and wait and hear nothing. Realize that they've moved on, and you, too, need to move on. It's not worth your time, and no amount of pestering them will change that.

IT'S A NO

If it's not a good fit, it's simply not a good fit. You may be contacted and informed that you didn't get the position. Say thank you, and tell them that you enjoyed getting to meet them. You *always* want to end things positively, because you've essentially done some networking with new people. Even if you aren't a right fit for that position, you never know what can come about in the future because of that meeting.

I once interviewed for a training position, and I thought the interview went well. The hiring manager called me to let me know that I was the second choice and that the position was going to someone else. I thanked her, told her I enjoyed getting to know her and her team, and said that I was confident that whoever they hired was very fortunate. I thought that would be the end of it and moved on. Less than two weeks later, I got a call from a completely different hiring manager from another company who said the hiring manager from the first company had called him, and she told him about me. He invited me for an interview, and I got the job! You *never* know what might come about.

Also, reflect on what you feel went right in the interview so that you can continue to improve in your next interview.

IT'S A YES

Well done! Clearly you impressed them in the interview, and you're that much closer to starting a new job. You now move along in the process, be it a second interview or straight to a job offer.

A SECOND INTERVIEW

Sometimes the process continues with a second interview, either with the same people or someone higher up in the organization. As with the phone interview or face-to-face interview, continue to develop CARs. Since this is a follow-up interview, you have more information about the job and the company, so you're not starting over from scratch. Prepare two or three questions about the role, based on your deeper understanding. When you go to the follow-up interview, don't assume anything. Be on your best behavior – the same rules still apply.

ACCEPTING THE JOB OFFER

You've been given a job offer, and you're ready to take it. When an offer is made, whether in person or over the phone, make sure you *clarify* and *verify*. Clarify any areas that you are unsure about, such as start date, getting a badge, where to park, etc. Verify the pay and benefits. You can choose at that point to say, "Yes, I accept, and I'm looking forward to starting," or "Thank you for the offer. I want to think it over tonight and get back with you with an answer tomorrow. Will that be acceptable?" The second choice is perfectly fine for some people and some positions. The employer has spent a great deal of time and money in recruiting and interviewing, and they are anxious to make the right decision, as they know you are. But it's okay to ask for time to think it over; a little more time won't kill them. This is a judgment call on your part. Do what's right for you.

. . . .

STARTING YOUR NEW JOB

. . . .

Congratulations! You made it to the finish line! Time to celebrate. If someone helped or encouraged you during your job search, reach out to them and thank them. Let them know what a difference their help and encouragement made.

When you first start your new job, refer to the notes you took during the interview. Also, ask lots of questions and take more notes.

I recommend that you make a list of your CARs throughout the year. This list can be used as a conversation starter for your annual performance review. I've done this several times throughout my career by sending the list of the year's CARs to my supervisor with a note, saying, "In preparing for my annual performance evaluation, here is a list of the things I've accomplished so far." I've had two different supervisors tell me they wished all their employees did that, because it helped them remember all the things that happened over the prior year.

Another benefit for keeping up with your CAR list is that you never know when you'll be interviewing again. It could be for another job within the same organization or with another company. If nothing else, you can look at your list periodically (as I do) for encouragement during those times at work when you feel like things aren't going so great. Focusing on what you did accomplish resets your mind and may get you going again in the right direction.

Chapter 11.
I Believe You Can Do This!

It was another cold afternoon on a Friday in late October, several years ago. We were initially hopeful that we would find someone as a good fit, since we had a large response to the open position. However, upon conducting interviews with the first few candidates, we were discouraged by the responses we were hearing.

Then, it all came together when someone with less experience than the previous candidates interviewed for the position. She answered our questions with specific examples, refrained from negative comments about her current or previous work, and showed a sincere interest in how she could help us solve our problems. We completed our interviews and hired her. She turned out to be even a better fit than we had hoped. She demonstrated the key elements that are presented in this book.

Looking for work is sometimes daunting and discouraging, and I've been where you are. When the U.S. economic recession hit around 2009, I was not immune. Work was difficult to find. I'd been on quite a few interviews and been a finalist several times but not selected.

I applied for one job, and was going in for series interviews. I was nervous because I really wanted to work, and jobs were so hard to find. Nevertheless, I followed the preparations that I've now outlined in this book, and I went in with the attitude of focusing on the people I was meeting, answering their questions, asking questions, and staying in the moment.

I got the job. I was told that I was up against some pretty stiff competition, but they liked the way I answered their questions with specific examples and that I asked good questions of them.

These two examples illustrate the impact of following what's been presented in this book. It's not hard. It doesn't compromise your integrity. If you have the willingness to do your best, equipped with the knowledge of how to conduct yourself, you will present the best *you* possible, and have a successful and productive interview.

If I can do it, you can do it. I believe that you can be successful if you are willing and genuine. I hope that you've found some encouragement and some helpful tools that will point you towards your next step. I sincerely wish you all the best on your career journey.

About The Author

 **GREG GILBERT** is an author, speaker, and career advisor with over 20 years of experience in corporate training and development, as well as career education and advising. He lives in Wichita, Kansas, with his wife, two children, and two cats. Greg loves coaching, educating, and inspiring others to find their right career path and to follow their strengths.

Learn more about Greg's current and upcoming Career Compass books and other career resources at www.CareerCompassBooks.com

Follow Greg the "Job Search Guy" on Google+ and YouTube and Career Compass on Facebook.

Thank You For Reading

I hope you enjoyed this book and found it helpful. If you did, please consider sharing it with others.

- Recommend this book to anyone who is going through a job search

- Mention the book in a Facebook post, Twitter update, Pinterest pin, or a blog post

- Visit www.facebook.com/CareerCompassBooks, "LIKE" and post a comment about what you enjoyed the most

- Get a copy for someone you know who would benefit from the book or send it as an Amazon gift

- Write a review on Amazon.com. Your support makes a huge difference - I read all the feedback myself, and I will use it to make this book and others even better.

Amazon   **Website**   **Facebook**